N ANIMALS

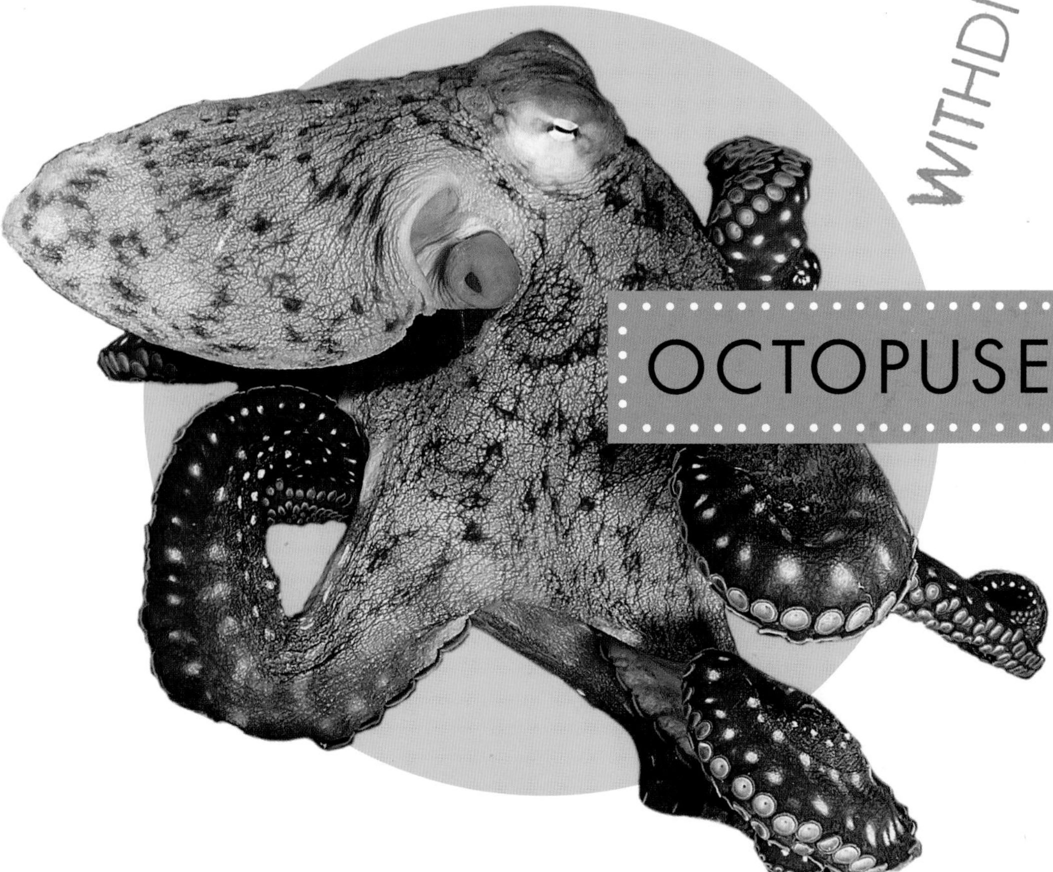

OCTOPUSES

by Mari Schuh

AMICUS | AMICUS INK

arms

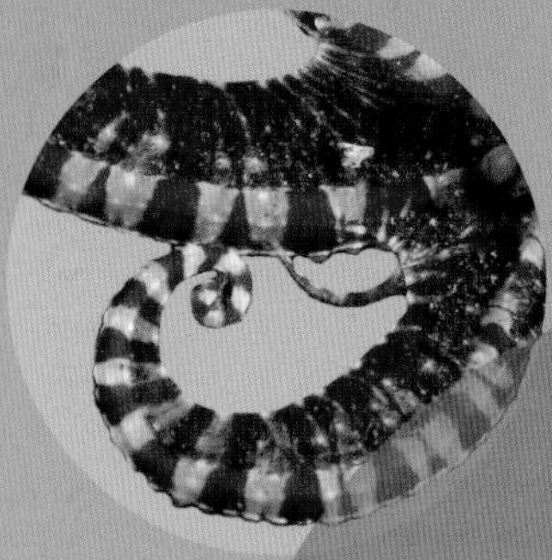

suckers

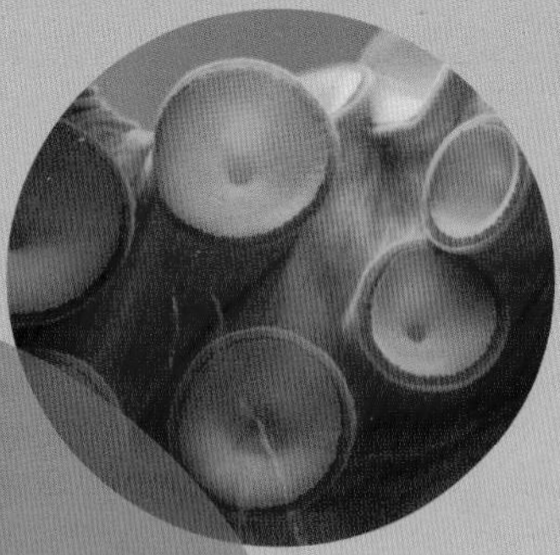

Look for these words and pictures as you read.

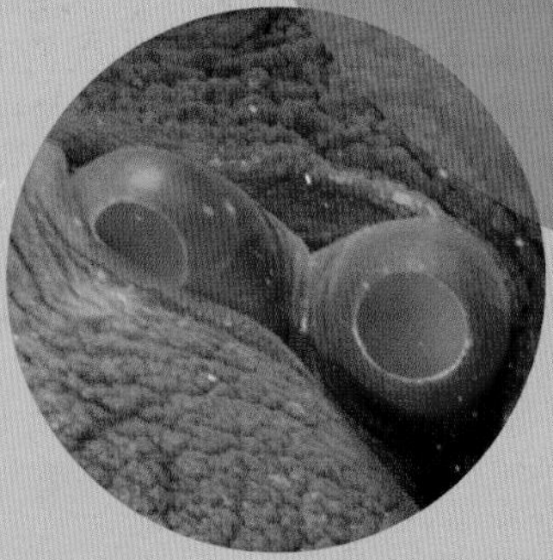

funnel

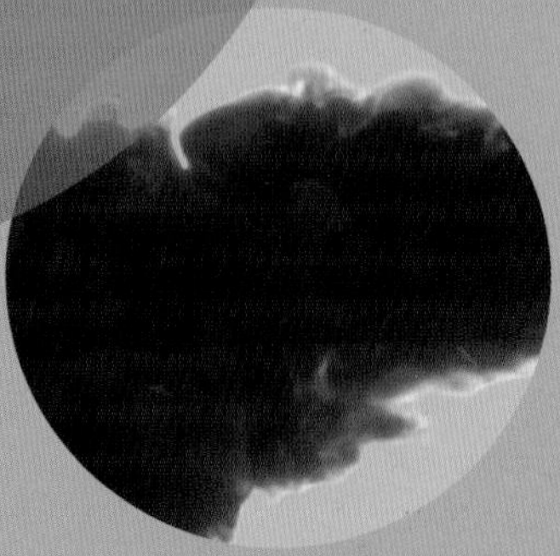

ink